A Nation Decides
The Scottish Referendum in Pictures

SUNSET UNDER THE FORTH ROAD BRIDGE.
by Stuart Sinclair

"This was taken just outside the lifeboat station in South Queensferry - I'd set up my DSLR for some long exposure shots but when I saw how beautiful the sunset was I captured this on my secondary (CSC) camera. This particular moment probably lasted about 60 seconds and then the sun set behind the hills. It was one of those in the right place at the right time moments. "

A Nation Decides

The Scottish Referendum in Pictures

compiled by Mark Barnes

The best way to take control over a people and control them utterly is to take a little of their freedom at a time, to erode rights by a thousand tiny and almost imperceptible reductions. In this way the people will not see those rights and freedoms being removed until past the point at which these changes cannot be reversed.

First published in 2014 in Great Britain by
i.Line Design - www.ilinedesign.com

This edition was published November 5th, 2014.

ISBN: 978-0-9929336-3-0

Available from http://ANationDecides.com

*For my mum, Shona, and
for the Love of Scotland,...
Saor Alba*

IRVINE... AT THE END OF THE PIER.
by Sharon Turnbull

"I love the journey that I'm on and I'm always learning. One time I can spend ages waiting patiently to capture a perfect sunset only to find that the sun has chosen that particular evening to be as unspectacular as possible, but another time I'll stumble across a beautiful ruin in a clearing in the woods somewhere and it just shouts out to be snapped. Anybody who takes their camera with them everywhere they go will know what I mean."

Fear Over Hope

a Bitter Battle

"First, supporters of independence will always be able to cite examples of small, independent and thriving economies across Europe such as Finland, Switzerland and Norway. It would be wrong to suggest that Scotland could not be another such successful, independent country.

David Cameron - Daily Telegraph - April 11th, 2007
www.telegraph.co.uk/comment/personal-view/3639114/Scots-and-English-flourish-in-the-Union.html

ONE QUESTION, ONE VOTE, ONE NATION

'I'm not suggesting that these Scottish parliamentarians who negotiated the Union weren't flawed. Yes, they were womanisers, drunkards and inconsistent. They were politicians - they also wanted to get to the top of the tree.

Christopher Whatley - Eminent Scottish Historian
www.theguardian.com/politics/2006/sep/24/uk.books

SCOTLAND'S FUTURE

YOUR GUIDE TO AN INDEPENDENT SCOTLAND

FREEDOM
by Sandra Proctor

Does freedom mean the same to you as freedom means to me?
Will freedom give us all the right to be who we can be?

To make our own decisions be they wrong or be they right
To choose just how we want to live will you join in the fight?

We send all of our taxes to the government down south
They give them back in pieces and we're living hand to mouth

They park their nuclear weapons right here on the River Clyde
They do not give a damn what happens to our countryside

They say 'Better Together' and for them that might be true
But that is only when you're looking from their point of view

From this side it seems to me they take more than they give
Leaving us with almost, but not quite, enough to live

If we are such a drain on them why not just let us go?
The truth is that they need us more than they will ever show

They hide from us the truth of things and feed us outright lies
For they know, that without them, it is Scotland who will rise

WAVES
by Dylan Walker

Facebook.com/IndependencePoems
www.dylanwalkerphotography.com

Margo MacDonald (19th April 1943 – 4th April 2014)

*"There will be harsh statements on both sides,
the debate will be fierce,
there will be verbal wounds inflicted...*

*...At one minute past ten on 18th September,
whatever the result,
she wanted those divisions to end
and this nation to seek a unity of purpose."*

"Personally I'm in favour of democracy, which means that the central institutions in the society have to be under popular control. Now, under capitalism we can't have democracy by definition. Capitalism is a system in which the central institutions of society are in principle under autocratic control. Thus, a corporation or an industry is, if we were to think of it in political terms, fascist; that is, it has tight control at the top and strict obedience has to be established at every level - there's a little bargaining, a little give and take, but the line of authority is perfectly straightforward. Just as I'm opposed to political fascism, I'm opposed to economic fascism. I think that until major institutions of society are under the popular control of participants and communities, it's pointless to talk about democracy."

Noam Chomsky
Business Today, May, 1973

PROFESSIONAL SPIN ...

VOTE NO
TO PROTECT
OUR PENSIONS

Just one poll on the risk of a 'yes' vote knocked billions off the value of Scottish companies, endangering the pensions of people in Scotland.

www.bettertogether.net

VOTE NO
TO PROTECT
SCOTTISH JOBS

1 million Scottish jobs are with companies based elsewhere in the UK or depend on exports there. Separation would put these jobs at risk.

www.bettertogether.net

VOTE NO
TO PROTECT
OUR NHS

The experts are clear. Leaving the UK would mean an extra £6 billion in cuts to public services like our NHS.

www.bettertogether.net

VOTE NO
TO KEEP
PRICES DOWN

Phone firms and supermarkets like Asda and Iceland have said that prices would rise if Scotland left the UK.

www.bettertogether.net

The difference between the highs & lows of North Sea oil tax revenue is **£11.9 billion** That's more than the entire NHS budget in Scotland.

The facts you need for the big decision — better together

Building ships for the UK Royal Navy sustains **4,000 Jobs** in Scots yards & many more in communities.

The facts you need for the big decision — better together

Our scientists, doctors & researchers receive **15%** of UK research funds - nearly double our population share.

The facts you need for the big decision — better together

Scots pay £320 million in licence fee but we get **£3.2 billion** of TV, radio & online content from our BBC in return.

The facts you need for the big decision — better together

As part of the United Kingdom the Pound is **our own currency** Our interest rates are not set by a foreign country.

The facts you need for the big decision — better together

Public spending in Scotland is **£1,200 higher per head** than the UK average.

The facts you need for the big decision — better together

Savers in Scotland benefit from a **£85,000** savings guarantee that pays out if your bank collapses

The facts you need for the big decision — better together

Scots savers have more than **2 Million ISAs** benefiting from UK tax relief.

The facts you need for the big decision — better together

"UK ministers are not going to fall into the trap of acting against Scotland <u>UNTIL</u> Scotland decides to stay in the UK."

Blair McDougall
Campaign Director of 'Better Together'

Straight from the horse's mouth. Westminster is waiting to spring that trap.

Yes to Independence
TIME TO BRING OUR GOVERNMENT HOME
Learn more at YesScotland.net

"Only independence can protect Scotland's NHS from Westminster privatisation"
Dr Harry Burns (Chief Medical Officer 2005 - 2014)

Yes

'The No campaign have no promises. They proclaim themselves "Better Together" but nowhere, in any piece of their literature, do they state how Scotland will be better by staying together. All they have ever promised is that Scotland will be worse on its own. Those two aren't quite the same thing. I'm voting Yes in the referendum, because when nothing is for certain, I think the possibility of better is better than the fear of worse.'

Alan from Partick
Friday, Aug 29 2014

More and more people are waking up to the great opportunities of Yes

Former Labour first minister
HENRY McLEISH
slams the negativity of No

"There are fear and scare stories... Next they'll be saying there will be seven years of famine in an independent Scotland and that aliens will land here"

Don't let them scare you. Scotland's got what it takes to be a successful, independent country.

Yes

Facebook.com/YesScotland   YesScotland.net

*"If Scotland does become Independent, this will have **NO EFFECT** on your State Pension. You will continue to receive it just as you do at present."*

DWP   Department for Work & Pensions.

Bedroom Tax
91%
of Scottish MPs voted against it
WESTMINSTER IMPOSED IT

Welfare Cuts
81%
of Scottish MPs voted against it
WESTMINSTER IMPOSED IT

VAT Increase
82%
of Scottish MPs voted against it
WESTMINSTER IMPOSED IT

Mail Sell-off
79%
of Scottish MPs voted against it
WESTMINSTER IMPOSED IT

Learn more at YesScotland.net

Yes to Independence
A better, fairer Scotland starts with Yes

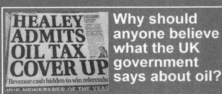

HEALEY ADMITS OIL TAX COVER UP
Revenue cash hidden to win referendum

Why should anyone believe what the UK government says about oil?

We're better off with Scotland's future in Scotland's hands **Yes**

RBS *The Royal Bank of Scotland*

"This is a technical procedure regarding the location of our registered head office. It is not our intention to move operations or jobs"
– Ross McEwan, RBS Chief Executive

The Nationalists will not guarantee that Arthur's Seat won't erupt in an independent Scotland

The only way to be sure Edinburgh won't be drowned in lava is to stay in the UK.

bettertogether
A stronger Scotland, a United Kingdom

SOME VERY SLICK CAMPAIGNING ...

ASK YOURSELF THIS...

If Scotland is the subsidy junky basket-case that westminster claims it is, why are they trying so hard to hang on to us?

It's almost as if we have something they want...

Only independence will give Scotland full control of its own resources.

WHAT WE TELL YOU:

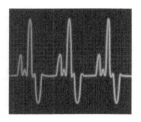

The difference between the highs & lows of North Sea oil tax revenue is **£11.9 billion**

That's more than the entire NHS budget in Scotland.

Source: HMRC & Scottish Government

The **facts** you need for the **big decision**   better**together**

"[North Sea oil] is a real jewel in the crown of the United Kingdom economy. I think what is encouraging is that this year we are seeing a growth in production as a number of new fields and projects come on stream."
David Cameron on North Sea oil at Prime Minister's Questions, 12 June 2013

"The Scottish Government is more or less out there on its own when being overly optimistic of the role oil can play".
Gavin Brown, Scottish Conservative Finance spokesman, STV News, 26 March 2013

Why do the No campaign say that oil would be a bad thing for an independent Scotland but a good thing for the Union?

Scotland's got what it takes ▶ **Yes**

WHAT WE LEFT OUT:

Without a penny of oil revenue, Scotland's GDP is still 99% of the UK average.

Oil money is a bonus to the Scottish economy, not a necessity.

It's just that it's a bonus big enough to pay for the entire Scottish NHS.

Source: HMRC and Scottish Government

project **fear**

"TO SUGGEST SOME SORT OF NEW OIL TAX REVENUE BOOM IS ABOUT TO EMERGE IS NOT READILY SUPPORTED BY THE EVIDENCE."
PROF JOHN MCLAREN & PROF JO ARMSTRONG
UNIVERSITY OF GLASGOW CENTRE FOR PUBLIC POLICY FOR REGIONS

 please **share**

better**together**

BBC — Sign in — News — Sport — Weather — iPlayer — TV — R

NEWS SCOTLAND BUSINESS

Home | World | UK | England | N. Ireland | Scotland | Wales | Business | Politics | Health | Education | Sci/E

Scotland Decides | Politics | Business | Edinburgh, Fife & East | Glasgow & West | Highlands & Islands

23 October 2014 Last updated at 20:18

28K — Share — f y ✉ ⎙

BP and GDF Suez discover new North Sea oil field

THINKSTOCK

Oil firms BP and GDF Suez have announced the discovery of a new field in the UK Central North Sea.

Related Stories

The find, which spans ... companies, has been ... day.

The discovery has be... Suez E&P UK, while B...

Scotland could be sitting on more than double the amount of oil and gas reserves currently predicted

How will they cope?

QUICK COMMERCIAL BREAK ...

Carlsberg don't do ██████s but if we did...

Carlsberg

Probably the biggest ██████ in the wor

A banker, a Daily Mail reader and a refugee are sitting at a table sharing 12 biscuits. The banker takes 11 and says to the Daily Mail reader: "Watch out for the refugee, he wants your biscuit!"

... LET ME ENTERTAIN YOU
by Stephen McBride featuring Johnnyguitar Twang

YES: GOOD FOR BUSINESS - I'LL DRINK TO THAT

Facebook.com/YesBarGlasgow

CALM, COOL, COLLECTED: TRÊS CHIC
by Keyser Soze featuring Stephanie Reilly and Nicola Sturgeon

FUR THE WEANS
by Maria Fawcett

We need tae say Yes fur the weans Ma,
tae see them safe and free.
But whit aboot ma pension lass,
so it's gotta be No fae me.

But yer pension will go up Ma,
jist you wait an' see,
Oh but how dae I know that's true lass,
So it's gotta be No fae me.

But whit aboot the weans Ma,
fur them we need tae say Yes.
Am too auld now to change lass,
So it's gotta be No fae me.

LEST WE FORGET
Our nation is one of caring, be that a moment or a lifetime...

THIS IS GORDON BROWN ...

The Trident programme is "unacceptably expensive, economically wasteful and militarily unsound" Gordon Brown MP, 1984

www.scotlandsaysyes.com

Cutting Corporation Tax might be Nationalist Policy, it might be Tory Policy but it is not and never was Labour Policy!

The Labour Party
Talking through its Anas

I cut it TWICE ye Numptie!

VOTE Yes GET RID

We'll give you more powers if you vote no but we won't tell you what they are and we won't tell you till next year.

I smell shite!

Yes I can definitely smell shite.

bettertogether

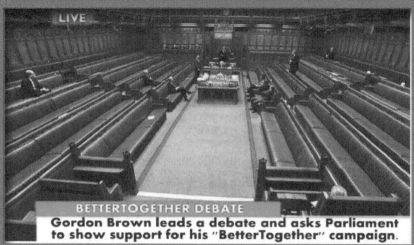

LIVE

BETTERTOGETHER DEBATE
Gordon Brown leads a debate and asks Parliament to show support for his "BetterTogether" campaign.

... HIS NICKNAME IS CLEARLY NOT DICK

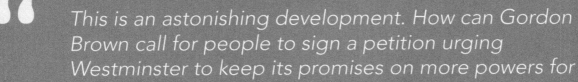

Dear Santa,
I have been a bad boy.
I made up a story that
scotland would get
lots n lots of new power
NOW I am in trouble.
Can you give scotland
those powers instead?
love
Gordon
x x x

"

This is an astonishing development. How can Gordon Brown call for people to sign a petition urging Westminster to keep its promises on more powers for Scotland when he himself has already said that is a vow which will be honoured?
He is now calling for guarantees on the delivery of something which he himself said during the referendum campaign was already a done deal.

Alex Salmond - Response to Gordon Brown Petition - September 30th, 2014
www.theguardian.com/politics/2014/sep/30/gordon-brown-david-cameron-scotland-trap

SOCIAL CREATIVITY AND HUMOUR ...

"Despite the historic symbolism and ironic original use of this image... I think it is wonderfully done, but just not a particularly clever message?"

"God Save The Queen... Anarchy In The UK... Is that Better Together?"

BT Supporters Facebook Comments

Dinnae bother... We'll dae It oorselves...

THESE ARE NOT BANKSY!

Hi Mark,

We don't feel comfortable giving permission for these images to be used, as they have been altered from their original state and it could be misleading.
We wont give permission for this, sorry.

Kind regards
faq@banksy.co.uk

THE YES CAMPAIGN ...

Facebook.com/TheYesYacht

... IS GATHERING PACE
by Alan Dodd

SUILVEN AND LOCH FIONN.
by John McCarthy (Lochinver Landscapes)

In recent years John has focused his attention on trying to capture the stunning scenery of Assynt and Coigach, a uniquely wild landscape in the far north west highlands with iconic mountains and hills standing proudly among countless glens and lochs. In 2012 John set up Lochinver Landscapes in the heart of the village of Lochinver to showcase his photography, as well as providing an outlet for other artists work

Soaring Spirits

a Flicker of Truth

In my 50 years of political reporting, I have known nothing like it. No campaign has been so historic, no vote has ever been so knife-edge and no result either way has ever been fraught with such danger and disastrous consequences.

Tom Brown - Daily Record - September 16th, 2014
www.dailyrecord.co.uk/news/politics/independence-referendum-how-dare-alex-4270679

"

If and when the Scots 'bottle it' on the 18th September and vote no, they will see a stronger English voice put them in their place. Because the people of England have had enough of Scottish self-interest.

"

Nigel Farage

FORGET FEAR, THIS IS SCARY

Are you thinking of voting no because of the "uncertainties" of independence?

Then you'd better be prepared to welcome what might be the UK's next coalition government.

Only an independent Scotland can guarantee that the people of Scotland get the government they voted for instead of one they didn't want. There's nothing uncertain about that!

VOTE YES.

DAD, LOOK OVER THERE ...
by Fearchara Fia

... OUR BRAVE WARRIORS ARE HERE

featuring Adam Waters

"The lines of the face are like the boughs of a tree, they bend and grow with wind, rain and blight. The wind is the life he had led, the rain like blood is his passion for his land and the blight has been the many failures of the past. Above them all however are his eyes, alive and twinkling with a hope no government can quash."

WE'RE RUNNING OUT OF SCARE STORIES. JUST SHUT UP AND VOTE NO.

independence might be hard, so let's not try to make anything better **together**

The head of the successful Better Together campaign today suggested Scotland might have voted for independence in last week's referendum if his campaign had made a positive case for the union, rather than "scaremongering" about economic risks..

Siraj Datoo - Buzzfeed - September 22nd, 2014
www.buzzfeed.com/sirajdatoo/better-together-campaign-chief-we-would-have-struggled-to-wi

KELLY MACDONALD
ON THE END OF BOARDWALK EMPIRE: MAGAZINE
GORDON STRACHAN
ON FACING THE WORLD CHAMPIONS: SPORT SECTION

sundayherald

7 September 2014

£1.30

51 49
YES SURGES AHEAD

Yes

YouGov poll shows independence support moves ahead of Better Together
PLUS: Panelbase poll shows increase in Yes support from women

THE MOVE TO YES ISSUE **IAN BELL** ON LABOUR **IAIN MACWHIRTER** ON THE MEDIA **VICKY ALLAN** ON THE ENGLISH IN SCOTLAND PLUS **FINTAN O'TOOLE** ON THE LESSONS OF IRELAND

The life and loves of Philip Larkin
BOOKS P.23

THE REVENGE OF A WOMAN SCORNED
TALKING POINTS P.25

"I am not what you expect a gay man to look like"
PEOPLE P.12

THE WEEK

13 SEPTEMBER 2014 | ISSUE 988 | £3.10 | THE BEST OF THE BRITISH AND INTERNATIONAL MEDIA

Please don't go
The last-ditch effort to save the Union
Page 6

FINGERS CROSSED FOR DEVO-MAX

"David Cameron , Ed Miliband and Nick Clegg have signed up to a historic joint statement that was demanded by the Daily Record on behalf of the people of Scotland."

David Clegg, Daily Record - September 15th, 2014 - www.dailyrecord.co.uk/news/politics/david-cameron-ed-miliband-nick-4265992

TUESDAY, SEPTEMBER 16, 2014

Daily Record

SCOTLAND'S SHAME · 55p

ONE NATION - TORIES DECIDE

THREE BAWBAGS SIGN PROMISE TO YOU JOCKS

Westminster's three party leaders – one of whom will be the next English Prime Minister in coalition with UKIP – sign a historic and meaningless bookie's slip which, in their own words, carries all the weight of a fart in a spacesuit and guarantees that, no matter what crap they come out with, we'll put it on our front page for you to be taken in...

Jim Murphy:
We must vote No for our expenses

Heartfelt plea from the MP for East Renfrewshire to save the Union – and his Westminster expenses of £252,916 in 2012-13 alone

SEE PAGES 6&7

FREE MILK
Available from your local food bank!

SEE PAGE 22

THE VOW

*T*he people of Scotland want to know that all three main parties from a foreign country will continue to exploit Scotland's natural resources to help with the UK's pitiful balance of payments. Accordingly,

WE ARE AGREED THAT:

The Scottish Parliament is permanent, at least until the October holiday, and extensive new powers will be delivered - to Westminster from Brussels when England votes to leave the European Union the year after next.

Your diddy Parliament will make way for a new ASDA superstore and it is our hope that the people of Scotland will remain as placid and punch-drunk as they have been for decades, thanks to the efforts of the Labour Party in delivering your vote - election after election - in return for a price freeze on family packs of tattie scones.

While the Scottish people remain part of the glorious and successful family of countries that make up this most United of Kingdoms, you will never be denied the opportunity to watch Dr Who. Or listen to The Archers. Or any of Nick Robinson's impartial political broadcasts.

Most importantly of all, people of Scotland, in the knowledge that we truly appreciate what is closest to your hearts, we pledge to you that we shall not sacrifice the United Kingdom's blue skies of freedom for the grey mists of a £12-a-pint Scottish republic.

RECORD VIEW · SIT DOWN, SHUT UP, VOTE NO AND KEEP ON CRINGING

THERE SHALL BE MORE POWERS FOR THE SCOTTISH PARLIAMENT

Power lies with the Scottish people and we believe it is for the Scottish people to decide how Scotland is governed.

We believe that the pooling and sharing of resources across the United Kingdom is to Scotland's benefit, in a partnership of four nations in which distinct national identities can flourish and be celebrated.

We believe that Scotland and the United Kingdom as a whole have been strengthened since the advent of devolution.

We support a strong Scottish Parliament in a strong United Kingdom and we support the further strengthening of the Parliament's powers.

The three parties delivered more powers for Holyrood through the Calman Commission which resulted in the Scotland Act 2012.

We now pledge to strengthen further the powers of the Scottish Parliament, in particular in the areas of fiscal responsibility and social security. We believe that Scotland should have a stronger Scottish Parliament while retaining full representation for Scotland in the UK Parliament. This can bring people together from all of Scotland, from civic society and every community.

The Scottish Labour Party, the Scottish Conservative and Unionist Party and the Scottish Liberal Democrats have each produced our own visions of the new powers which the Scottish Parliament needs.

We shall put those visions before the Scottish people at the next general election and all three parties guarantee to start delivering more powers for the Scottish Parliament as swiftly as possible in 2015.

We will deliver a stronger Scottish Parliament in a stronger United Kingdom.

Johann Lamont — Leader of the Scottish Labour Party

Ruth Davidson — Leader of the Scottish Conservative & Unionist Party

Willie Rennie — Leader of the Scottish Liberal Democrats

Ed Miliband — Leader of the Labour Party

David Cameron — Leader of the Conservative Party

Nick Clegg — Leader of the Liberal Democrats

NO THANKS

HERE'S WHAT YOU'RE ACTUALLY GUARANTEED IF YOU VOTE NO:

THE MORE
POWERS FOR SCOTLAND
ARGUMENT
EXPLAINED USING A BANANA

THIS IS A BANANA

VOTE NO AND I MIGHT GIVE YOU 40% OF THE BANANA

VOTE YES AND I WILL GIVE YOU THE WHOLE BANANA

(40% OF THE BANANA IS THE SKIN AND PRETTY USELESS TO YOU)

The Scots people are not daft and we will question Alex Salmond's vision, but we're not going to have wool pulled over our eyes by a 'NO' fear campaign. Both sides need to set out their vision for what Scotland looks like in ten, twenty years and provide the evidence base to justify those claims.

Sir Tom Hunter. Scottish businessman, entrepreneur and philanthropist
Reaction to the release of "Scotland's Future: Your guide to an independent Scotland"

You don't listen! The referendum is NOT about Alex Salmond..... ARRRGGH!

Yes

WE'RE DONE WITH THE ...

"*Bias takes many forms. It is at its most insidious when it's hidden. The BBC's is – as Andrew Marr put it – a 'cultural liberal bias… it's a publicly funded, urban organisation with an abnormally large number of young people, ethnic minorities and gay people.'*"

Stephen Pollard, Telegraph - October 24th, 2014 - http://bit.ly/10bTsCH

BBC

... BIAS, BILE & CRAP

"The BBC's bias – or disposition, if you want a less pejorative word – isn't conscious.
But we all bring our own dispositions to the work we do, and that's as true of BBC
journalists as it is of lawyers and plumbers. The BBC's news simply reflects the
mindset of its urban, culturally liberal staff."

WHAT A WEEK.
by Billy Kilpatrick

These images from the last few days leading up to the vote capture the last minute surge of support for the YES campaign in Glasgow.

13 / 10/ 2014

16 / 10/ 2014

17 / 10 / 2014

THE SKY'S THE LIMIT.
by Gail Ross

THE CALM BEFORE THE STORM

Finger Painting #4 by Wee Skribbles

NEW POWERS TO BE PROMISED TO SCOTLAND

- Special glasses that you put on and you see everyone naked.

- Unlimited Kate Bush tickets.

- A night with the spouse of any member of the cabinet / shadow cabinet like in that film with Robert Redford.

- The power to always find a parking spot right by wherever you're going.

- 1 royal baby every year.

- Invisibility.

- A blank ID like in Doctor Who that you hold up and people see whatever you want them to see.

- The ability to change shape into an animal of your choice (1 animal per person)

- Telepathy (not to be used on politicians)

- Immunity to hangovers.

- The power to go back in time and rectify up to 3 mistakes you've made in your life.

- A weekly massage from any member of the cabinet (includes happy ending)

- The ability to control other people purely with the power of your mind.

- Sexual irresistibility.

- Immortality

- All You Can Eat for a year at Nando's

ALL POWERS TO BE IN PLACE WITHIN 2 DAYS OF A NO VOTE

@DavidSchneider
DaveSchneider.co.uk

THE LAST DAY OF THE CAMPAIGN ...
by Alan Dodd

DARKNESS DESCENDS ...
by Tony Clerkson

IS THAT THUNDER ON THE HORIZON?

by Tommy Gilmour

"

There must be 3,000 Scots in Glasgow's George Square who are celebrating like they have won the World Cup. The atmosphere is one of joyous celebration.

"

Christopher Hope – Telegraph – September 18th, 2014

LAGGAM DAM.
by Dana De Art

Dana first picked up a camera in 2013 and in a very short space of time became a professional published photographer. She is particularly creative and has a particular passion for colour and capturing moments in time. She loves to point her lens at anything from landscapes, wildlife, people or the night sky. She particularly enjoys letting her creative side go wild experimenting with portraits.

A Nation Divided

Shattered Illusions

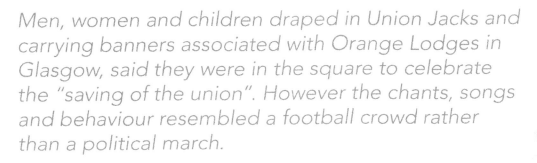

"Men, women and children draped in Union Jacks and carrying banners associated with Orange Lodges in Glasgow, said they were in the square to celebrate the "saving of the union". However the chants, songs and behaviour resembled a football crowd rather than a political march.

Chris Green, James Cusick - The Independent - September 19th, 2014
www.independent.co.uk/news/uk/home-news/9745333.html

WE'RE BETTER TOGETHER
by Jon Brady

"Hello! I'm Jon Brady – a Scottish photographer, games and music writer and oddjob profiteer based in Glasgow.
I like big cameras, big lenses, videogames, music, film, a good interview and the buzz of being up for 20 hours longer than I'm meant to. I've got experience in photography and photo editing and extensive experience writing about videogames, music and film for a number of online blogs. I help film the occasional video too and once I managed to sit all the way through Only God Forgives without leaving the cinema."

"Dozens of rival Unionists and independence supporters have gathered in George Square, in the centre of Glasgow, where they were being separated by police.
A spokeswoman for Police Scotland said there were about 100 people in each of the two groups, and although there had been some "minor disorder" it had been dealt with quickly by officers."

BBC News Scotland - September 19th, 2014
www.bbc.co.uk/news/uk-scotland-29287409

"
INDEPENDENCE HAS BEEN PUT TO BED
"

"So, just as Scotland will vote separately in the Scottish Parliament on their issues of tax, spending and welfare so too England, as well as Wales and Northern Ireland, should be able to vote on these issues and all this must take place in tandem with, and at the same pace as, the settlement for Scotland."

David Cameron - September 19th, 2014

MEDIA MANIPULATION ...

Tafalgar Square: Thousand's rally & gather to save the NHS from privatisation. 'Scottish' Labour tell Scots this ain't happening.

Daily Record
SCOTLAND'S CHAMPION

ALISTAIR DARLING BETTER TOGETHER

From politicians to pundits, celebrities to the man and woman in the street, we say this vote is a test of common sense, not a test of Scottishness. So just say.

NO THANKS

What's ruining YOUR love life? FOUR-PAGE SPECIAL PULLOUT INSIDE

Scottish Daily Mail

Salmond and the secret plans for £2m castle
EXCLUSIVE: PAGES 6&7

- Mail poll on eve of vote puts Yes on 48pc and No on 52pc
- Miliband abused as row over bullying tactics intensifies
- Business braced for shares crisis if Scotland backs split

24 HOURS TO SAVE BRITAIN

DAILY EXPRESS
THE WORLD'S GREATEST NEWSPAPER

FREE INSIDE
HISTORIC DAILY EXPRESS EDITION
EDWARD VIII ABDICATES
...AND ALL THIS WEEK COLLECT REPRINTS OF THE AMAZING EVENTS THAT CHANGED THE WORLD

OUTRAGE AT BRIBES FOR SCOTS

Politicians pledge more of your cash to save the Union

Police hunt mystery prowler over murder of Thai beach Britons

Propoganda Machine
Yes, No, Unsure?
Same Day, Same Newspaper, Differemt Country, Different "Truth"

DAILY EXPRESS
A TOUCHING FAREWELL TO PEACHES GELDOF | END OF THE ROAD FOR UNITED BOSS MOYES

PENSION SHOCK FOR MILLIONS
New warnings over a massive drop in income

TV STAR SUSANNA STRICTLY PREPARED ME FOR ANYTHING

What the Express said to English readers

What the Express said to Scottish readers

Scottish DAILY EXPRESS
A TOUCHING FAREWELL TO PEACHES GELDOF | END OF THE ROAD FOR UNITED BOSS MOYES

PENSIONS SAFER WITHIN THE UK
Annual bill would be three times Scots oil income, says Brown

Yes

You can decide
18th Sept 2014

WHY DON'T WE TELL THE SCOTS TO SHOVE OFF!

Muslim pals of Alan in I.S. plea

AS SCOTLAND DECIDES..

NOS AHEAD BY A NOSE

EXCLUSIVE RIO

BETTER TOGETHER
Harry back with ex lover Cressida

SCOTTISH **DAILY EXPRESS**
WE'RE BETTER TOGETHER

DON'T LET THE SUN SET ON OUR UNION

SCOTS have been urged to reject 'narrow nationalism' and save the Union in today's historic referendum.

SCOTLAND'S DAY OF DECISION: PAGES 2&3 ● CAMPAIGNS REACH FEVER PITCH: PAGES 4&5 ● COMMENT: PAGE 12

... GLORIA GAYNOR WAS APPALLED

by Mark Barnes

At first I was afraid I was petrified
Kept reading the Daily Record believing all their lies
But then I woke up on the 19th, realising how they did me wrong
And I grew wise and decided to rewrite this song

And so we're back from freedom square
I just walked in to find you here so I've piled you over there
I should have cancelled my delivery, I should have put you in the trash
If I had known for just one second, you'd be lying next to me

Go on now go, you try to sell
Just keep a lookout, cause you're gonna burn in hell
Weren't you the one who tried to cheat me with your lie
Did you think I'd crumble, did you think I'd lay down and die?

But as for me. I'm doing great
I buy the Herald, gives me good news on a plate,
I've met some great folks and they're only 45
They've cheered me up, now it's great to be alive

The fear is gone, I'm out to fight,
I'm gonna burn ma Daily Records and rid me o their shite
I'm gonna invite roond a' the neebours, build a bonfire oot the back,
with a' ma Daily Records, going a' the way back.

EDINBURGH - 2 DAYS AFTER THE VOTE

SURPRISE
by Sandra Proctor

Well, would you believe it?
Now there's a surprise!
It turns out Westminster's
Been telling us lies

They're not really going to give
Scotland more powers
They don't have to now
We have given up ours

We gave up our rights
And we've no-one to blame
Except for ourselves
And that is Scotland's shame

Facebook.com/IndependencePoems
HeinzKochPhotography.com

BY YON BONNIE BANKS

by Heinz Koch

the ice queen stands on one tree hill
this time she stands alone
the mist may hide the mountain tops
but can never hide the shame
of too many scottish souls who didnt feel the same ...

the heather's red with labour lies
though not a man was slain
but still a nation died inside
and nothing will be the same again

we sang and danced with flag in hand
in towns and cities across this land
we now gather with shopping bags
to feed those who do not have

through tv sets and media
they turned each against our own
now thanks to fear and false promises
how many old folk can heat their homes

hunger cold and poverty
now rule this land of mine
greed and selfish manners
traits I cannot stand !

I give my heart today
to the country that I love
and hope one day that we'll be free
as intended by god above

until that day I'll do my best
to watch these evil men
and fight their greedy ways
with paper and my pen ....

ICE QUEEN DOESN'T USUALLY HAVE TITLES.

a Poem by Debs MacDonald

TUESDAY, SEPTEMBER 16, 2014

Daily Record

SCOTLAND'S SHAME · 55p

THREE BAWBAGS SIGN PROMISE TO YOU JOCKS

Westminster's three party leaders – one of whom will be the next English Prime Minister in coalition with UKIP – sign a historic and meaningless bookie's slip which, in their own words, carries all the weight of a fart in a spacesuit and guarantees that, no matter what crap they come out with, we'll put it on our front page for you to be taken in...

Jim Murphy: We must vote No for our expenses

Heartfelt plea from the MP for East Renfrewshire to save the Union – and his Westminster expenses of £252,916 in 2012-13 alone

SEE PAGES 6&7

FREE MILK
Available from your local food bank!

SEE PAGE 22

O' Vow For Scotland
by @SirEdHilarious

O' Vow for Scotland; When will we see, those pow'rs we'd gain?
That people crossed "No" for, And denied their nation in pen.
And Brown stood up for them, Proud Westminster's army;
And then they went homeward...... Ne'er seen again.

The Vow is bare now; And Westminster lies, so soon exposed.
Empty promises lost now, Of Miliband, Cam'ron and Clegg.
And Brown stood up for them, Proud Westminster's army;
And then they went homeward...... Ne'er seen again.

Those pow'rs are gone now; And in the past, they will remain.
For they were just lies meant, To save the Union again.
And Brown stood up for them, Proud Westminster's army;
And then they went homeward...... Ne'er seen again.

RECORD VIEW **SIT DOWN, SHUT UP, VOTE NO AND KEEP ON CRINGING**

IT'S NO LAUGHING MATTER

COMIC RELIEF

Bridges' £1k food bank gift

I've been gagging to help

By BEN ARCHIBALD

COMIC Kevin Bridges came to the rescue of a food bank running low on supplies — by personally turning up with £1,000 of vouchers to buy meals.

Kind-hearted Kevin, 27, appeared at the charity's offices with the huge bundle of Tesco tokens after a Twitter picture of their empty shelves went viral.

And Julie Webster, 38, founder of the centre in Maryhill, Glasgow, told how she was so stunned when she heard about the star's generosity she thought it was a wind-up.

She said: "I got a call to say Kevin was in the store. My reaction was 'Aye right', but I was passed the phone and he said how disappointed he was to miss me.

"He'd asked the staff how much it would take to fill all the shelves and they said £1,000 and he went to Tesco and bought them." Work-

Thanks Kev . . . staff with trolley supplies

ers later tweeted Kev a snap of three trolleys of food bought with last Friday's donation. He replied: "A pleasure. Well done to you and all the volunteers. Great work."

Julie — whose volunteers feed 200 people a week — revealed the comedian wasn't the only famous face to help them out.

Scottish Sun columnist and Celtic star Kris Commons' wife Lisa Hague also handed over supplies last week.
ben.archibald@the-sun.co.uk

@Maryhillbank
All thanks to YOU Kevin Bridges you have stopped sleepless nights worrying about not having enough food THANK YOU

@KevinBridges86
No problem. Well done to you and all the volunteers. Great work

Father and son Andrew and Darren Carnegie from Glasgow's Needy Foodbank would like to say a massive thank you to everyone who donated so generously to their foodbank collection in George Square the past two weekends.
The organisation received donations worth nearly £50,000 over the past few weeks.

The Genn - October 3rd, 2014
thegenn.co.uk/thank-you-glasgows-needy/

GLASGOW'S NEEDY

Glasgow's Needy Needs Your Help!

Tinned Food

Dried Food

Cereals

Sauces

Unopened toiletries

Other Stuff

This is not a charity. It's Humanity

Andrew Carnegie 07584 626 557
Darren Carnegie 07887 492 034

andrewcarnegie69@hotmail.co.uk
darrencarnegie@hotmail.com
www.facebook.com/glasgowsneedy
@darrencarnegie

INNOCENCE.
by Carly Campbell

For more photographs visit Facebook.com/CarlyCampbellPhotography

"There's something special about photographs. Not just that they capture moments as they happen, but they can help people see the beauty in something they might not have ever noticed. Everyone is so busy going about their day to day lives and they sometimes forget to stop and appreciate the little things. A single photograph has the power to change someone's mind, let them see the light at the end of the tunnel and reassure them that not everything is as dark and dreary as it may seem.."

Hope Over Fear

Onwards and Upwards

The true guardians of progress are not the political parties at Westminster, or the parties here at Holyrood – they are the energised electorate of this nation, one which is speaking loud and clear. All of us must realise that things cannot ever be the same again.

Alex Salmond - First Minister Statement - September 23rd, 2014
news.scotland.gov.uk/Speeches-Briefings/First-Minister-statement-1076.aspx

"Scotland is, I think, for the whole of mankind an inspiring example of a country inhabited by people basing their nationality on civic rather than ethnic identity."

Sir John Davies
Historian

EIGHT GROYNES
by Dylan Walker

ABERDEEN RALLIES FOR HOPE OVER FEAR

by Ivon Bartholomew

SOME THINGS ARE WORTH FIGHTING FOR ...

When things go wrong, as they sometimes will,
When the road you're trudging seems all uphill,
When funds are low and the debts are high,
And you want to smile but you have to sigh,
When care is pressing you down a bit,
Rest if you must, but don't you quit.

Life is queer with its twists and turns,
As every one of us sometimes learns,
And many a failure turns about,
When he might have won if he'd stuck it out.
Don't give up, though the pace seems slow -
You may succeed with another blow.

Success is failure turned inside out -
The silver tint of the clouds of doubt,
And you never can tell how close you are -
It may be near when it seems afar;
So stick to the fight when you're hardest hit -
It's when things seem worst that you mustn't quit.

O' FLOWER OF SCOTLAND
Inspiration courtesy of Pat Plunkett

This sums up the generation looking forward so ours can have a better life. The wise eyes si full of hope fir a future she wint enjoy ... thank you Pat for all your errfort a life long battle will soon be done, Yer friends on FB xx

O flower of Scotland
When will we see your like again
That fought and died for
Your wee bit hill and glen
And stood against him
Proud Edward's army
And sent him homeward
Tae think again

The hills are bare now
And autumn leaves lie thick and still
O'er land that is lost now
Which those so dearly held
And stood against him
Proud Edward's army
And sent him homeward
Tae think again

Those days are passed now
And in the past they must remain
But we can still rise now
And be the nation again
That stood against him
Proud Edward's army
And sent him homeward
Tae think again

YOUR NUMBER'S UP.
by Stephen McBride

"A new Ipsos Mori survey for STV shows that support for the SNP has surged to 52%, giving them a projected 54 seats at Westminster."

http://www.businessforscotland.co.uk/no-campaign-parties-in-general-election-meltdown/

THE LION AWAKENS.
based entirely on artwork by Jon Edwards

This image is a recreation entirely based on original artwork created by Jon Edwards

"This iconic backdrop was originally created by Jon Edwards and was subsequently adapted and reused by numerous social media groups and pages. Despite attempts to contact Jon Edwards for permission to use his original image, this was not possible. This is the closest I could get to recreating his work as faithfully as I could"

WHO'S LAUGHING NOW ...

THE 3 STOOGES

The Tories:
Introducing the
new 19th Century

The end of welfare

Poverty

Crime

Homelessness

Profit before people

Healthcare:
Pay up or die

Hunger   Elitism

False morality

Political corruption

Workfare

GOD SAVE THE QUEEN
The Conservatives New Victorian Britain

JANUARY 2014

NIGEL FARAGE
SAYS IT WOULD BE
"RIDICULOUS" TO
PROTECT THE
NHS FROM
SPENDING CUTS

OCTOBER 2014

NIGEL FARAGE
LAUNCHES A
POSTER CLAIMING
**"ONLY UKIP
WILL PROTECT
OUR NHS"**

NIGEL FARAGE: JUST MAKING IT UP AS HE GOES ALONG

Please do not break this family apart. (That's our job)

They wage war on their own people, they use mass surveillance to spy on them, they use forced labour schemes, they have absolute contempt for freedom of the press, they manipulate the justice system by rewriting any law that constrains them from doing whatever the hell they like, they impoverish whole communities and starve regions of investment, all in order to preserve the wealth for their inner circle.

No, this isn't North Korea, it's the United Kingdom under Tory rule.

ANOTHER ANGRY VOICE

CAMERON	MILIBAND	CLEGG	FARAGE	BENNETT	
					**ANOTHER ANGRY VOICE**
CONSERVATIVES PRO-AUSTERITY ANTI-MONETARY REFORM ANTI-RENATIONALISATION ANTI-ELECTORAL REFORM PRO-TTIP	**LABOUR** PRO-AUSTERITY ANTI-MONETARY REFORM ANTI-RENATIONALISATION ANTI-ELECTORAL REFORM PRO-TTIP	**LIB-DEMS** PRO-AUSTERITY ANTI-MONETARY REFORM ANTI-RENATIONALISATION PRO-ELECTORAL REFORM PRO-TTIP	**UKIP** PRO-AUSTERITY ANTI-MONETARY REFORM ANTI-RENATIONALISATION NO CLEAR ELECTORAL REFORM POLICY NO CLEAR TTIP POLICY	**GREEN PARTY** ANTI-AUSTERITY PRO-MONETARY REFORM PRO-RENATIONALISATION PRO-ELECTORAL REFORM ANTI-TTIP	
☑ INVITED TO THE LEADERS' DEBATES BY THE MAINSTREAM MEDIA	☑ INVITED TO THE LEADERS' DEBATES BY THE MAINSTREAM MEDIA	☑ INVITED TO THE LEADERS' DEBATES BY THE MAINSTREAM MEDIA	☑ INVITED TO THE LEADERS' DEBATES BY THE MAINSTREAM MEDIA	☑ NOT INVITED TO THE LEADERS' DEBATES BY THE MAINSTREAM MEDIA	

"The smart way to keep people passive and obedient is to strictly limit the spectrum of acceptable opinion, but allow very lively debate within that spectrum." Noam Chomsky

Cassetteboy's remix of Cameron's conference speech is blowing up on Twitter

One commentator called it 'the only version of Cameron's speech worth watching'.

METRO.CO.UK

MISSING

HAVE YOU SEEN GORDON?

Described as an "ex-politician", Gordon Brown was last seen on Sept 14th stating . .

"The UK will move as close to federalism as we can go in a country where one nation accounts for 80% of the population."

If you've seen Gordon, please contact the Tories who are very anxious to have him on TV again to deflect voters from 'The Vow' back-peddling.

Indyscot

Speak Up for Scotland: Vote SNP for Westminster 2015 Vote pro-Indy for Holyrood 2016.

MISSING

Johann Lamont
Last seen in Falkirk area. Known to be in a confused and deluded state. If you have any information, please contact her guardian, Mr Miliband: 0845 0922299

RUSSELL BRAND SAYS 'IF YOU WANT A DAFT COMEDIAN RUNNING LONDON, JUST LEAVE THINGS AS THEY ARE'

Vote Yes

Join the campaign for an **independent London**

RUN PRIME MINISTER, RUN... **BUT YOU CAN'T HIDE** 2015

LEGAL AID CUTS · ATOS · UNEMPLOYMENT · PAY FREEZE · NHS PRIVATISATION · GREED · DISABLISM · ROYAL MAIL SELL OFF · CUTS · IMPS PAY RISE · DISCRIMINATION · NHS PRIVATISATION · FOODBANKS · STUDENT FEES · POVERTY · WORKFARE · FREE SCHOOLS · BANKERS BONUSES · STUPIDITY · ZERO HOURS CON · LOSS OF EMPLOYMENT RIGHTS · CORRUPTION

REALITY IS GAINING ON YOU

MAGNIFICENT GLENCOE.
by John Hastings

"I have had a camera in my hand since I was a teenager and I think of myself as an photographer with a wide ranging portfolio. Living in East Kilbride in Central Scotland, I am within easy reach of dramatic coastlines, majestic mountains or urban landscapes. A photographer with a personal style, interested in looking at the overlooked"

Scotlands Future

Dedicated Tae The Weans

"The following images are dedicated to Scotland's real future, our children. They will live with the decisions we have made and the decisions we have yet to make. Politics continues to deny Scotland a fair chance at independence and in the process denies our children the chance to be truly free..."

Mark Barnes - October 14th, 2014

FREE, SCOTTISH AND PROUD
by Charlie McAulay Robertson

Gathered the children, that are of our creation,
Made up of every religious and ethnic persuasion,
The corner stone of our Scottish nation,
They will be our country's true salvation.

They have our future firmly in their hand,
On our behalf, will make a stand,
Justice for us, they will demand,
And won't stop, till the mountains turn to sand.

They won't be bought and they won't be cowed,
As their blood is strong and their voices loud.
Never again will our nations heads be bowed,
We will be Free, Scottish and Proud.

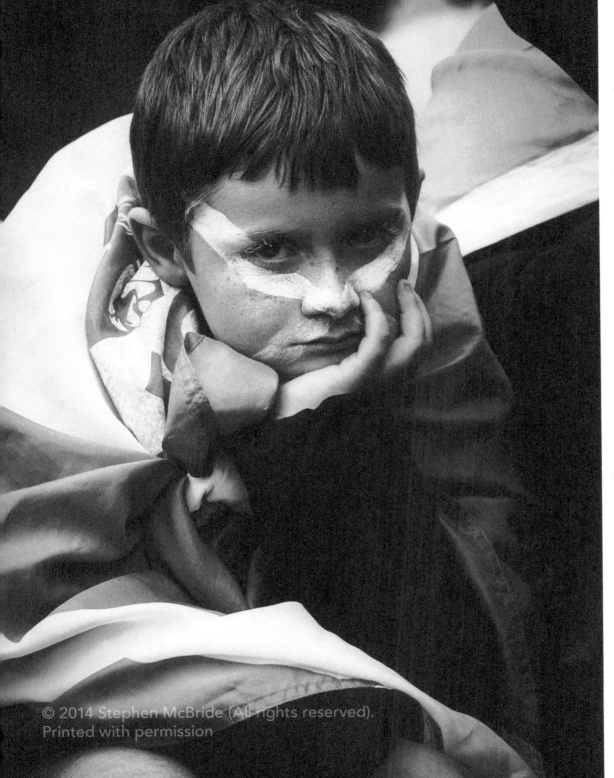

THE EYES NEVER LIE.
by Stephen McBride

One day soon Sam you will smile, you are my inspiration to carry on campaigning for Independence. x

Today is a new day. Thank God. Yesterday was worse.
I feel so mixed up. And so let down.

Right now, I feel as though this country that I was so proud of
has just thrown away its soul.

Scotland was centre stage. The show was about to begin
and the rest of the world was watching, with excitement
and anticipation. There was tangible hope in the air.

I truly believed that this proud and confident nation of ours
was going to show the world how to create a caring, tolerant
society, which has integrity as its soul.

For a moment, that dream was tangible. We were going to show
the world that it is possible to reject self-interest and greed,
in favour of a new way of doing things. A future full of hope
and promise and built on fairness and true empowerment.

I was sharing this new awakening of national hope
with many, many others.

A new Scottish Enlightenment was a tangible option.

So, some people got stage fright. It is hardly surprising.
There was so much fear being spread around and some
of it was bound to get into people's heads and hearts.

Sadly, much of that fear had been deliberately planted
there by others, hell-bent on sabotaging this new hope,
in favour of their own, selfish aims.

On this new day, it feels to me like they have won
and the show is over.

That dream has now left the building.

Or has it?

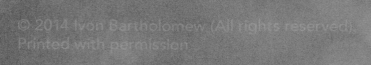

Walking home from the polling station two days ago, with
five-year-old Holly and three-year-old Finlay, we took
a hopeful shortcut through our beautiful, shared garden.

When we got to our favourite picnic spot, we discovered
a huge clearing there, where once had stood our majestic,
two hundred-year-old elm.

I was told, though, by the good men there who had brought
it down, that it had been infected with Dutch Elm Disease
and had to go.

All that now remained of it were the smouldering embers.

The significance, supremely poignant at that moment,
on that day, of all historic days, was not lost on me.

I had just voted for Holly and Finlay's future;
for empowerment, democracy and peaceful change
and I still do have faith in the good people of Scotland
to make it happen.

So let us not just throw ourselves to the lions here, nor fall
on our swords.

Let us unite, be strong and address what is rotten
at the core of our nation.

We can still change this country, for the better and forever.

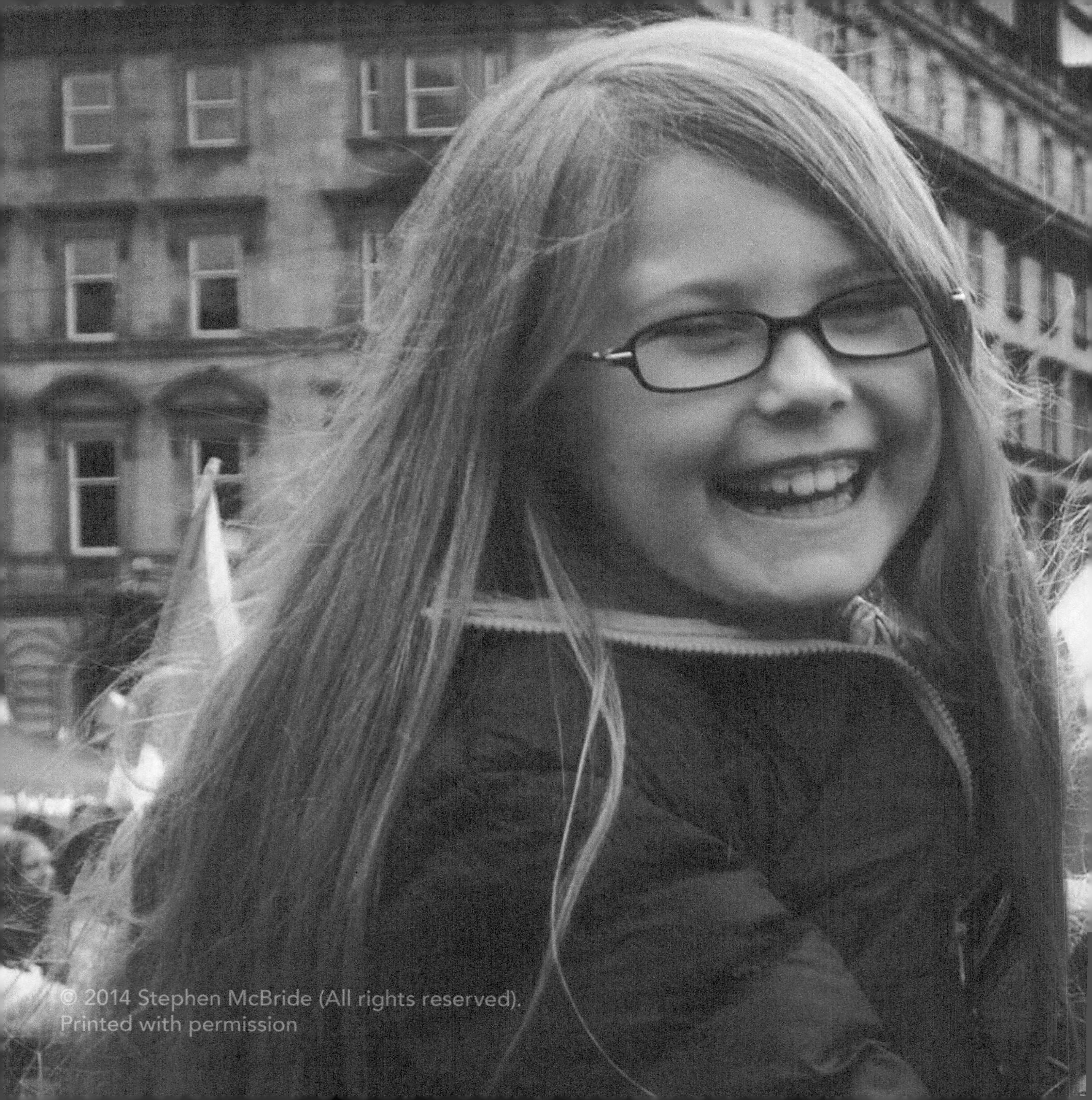

HOLLY'S LULLABY
by Stephen McBride

Don't be frightened my little one
I'll keep you sheltered from the rain
I know you hear a noise outside
It's just the hailstones on the pane

The wind it whistles up the close
But it's just a sound, it's not a ghost
Daddy will keep you safe from harm
Don't fret my child don't be alarmed

No reason now why you can't sleep
Shut your eyes and count the sheep
Your Daddy's here I'll always be
Your story told your hand to hold

I'll comfort you and hold you close
I'll kiss your cheek and tuck you in
You're all I think I ever wanted
Just never knew it till you landed

Beautiful little perfect girl
You tiny toes and fingers curled
And everyday I watched you grow
I want so much for you and more

So wrap up warm hold monkey tight
I'll draw the curtains dim the light
And if you wake up with a fright
I'll fight your monsters, be your knight

THE REFERENDUM KIDS.

by Kenneth Falconer and Stephen McBride

Sean, when I saw the disappointment on your face, I became more determined than ever to never give up the fight for Independence. Love Dad. x

Alana and Matthew. You are my future and Scotland's future. You have the power and passion to change the world. I love you so much and could not be more proud. Love Mummy & Paige xxx

Danielle & Tayven, you are the reason why we fight, you are the reason why I fight. It's all for you & my pride for you runs so deep, my little freedom fighters. All my love always Mummy. X

IF ONLY
by Ivon Bartholomew, featuring Finlay

IF

If you can keep your head when all about you
    Are losing theirs and blaming it on you,
If you can trust yourself when all men doubt you,
    But make allowance for their doubting too;
If you can wait and not be tired by waiting,
    Or being lied about, don't deal in lies,
Or being hated, don't give way to hating,
    And yet don't look too good, nor talk too wise:

If you can dream - and not make dreams your master;
    If you can think - and not make thoughts your aim;
If you can meet with Triumph and Disaster
    And treat those two impostors just the same;
If you can bear to hear the truth you've spoken
    Twisted by knaves to make a trap for fools,
Or watch the things you gave your life to, broken,
    And stoop and build 'em up with worn-out tools:

If you can make one heap of all your winnings
    And risk it on one turn of pitch-and-toss,
And lose, and start again at your beginnings
    And never breathe a word about your loss;
If you can force your heart and nerve and sinew
    To serve your turn long after they are gone,
And so hold on when there is nothing in you
    Except the Will which says to them: 'Hold on!'

If you can talk with crowds and keep your virtue,
    Or walk with Kings -nor lose the common touch,
If neither foes nor loving friends can hurt you,
    If all men count with you, but none too much;
If you can fill the unforgiving minute
    With sixty seconds' worth of distance run,
Yours is the Earth and everything that's in it,
    And - which is more - you'll be a Man, my son!

Rudyard Kipling

www.IvonBartholomew.com

As this is the final image in the book by Ivon, I wanted to say a special thank you to him for all the fantastic photos he provided for the book. Only a small fraction of those donated were eventually used.

Max, we loved it when you told Nicola Sturgeon your joke
"What wobbles in the sky? A Jellycopter!"
Love you, Mummy and Daddy xxx

Amelia-Rose the future is in your hands, be everything you can be and more!! Love yi always mum and dad x

To Eilidh, Dylan, Cole and Owen,

Be the change you want to see in the world.

Always believe in yourselves.

Love Mum and Dad x

We would like to say a big thanks to our kids Craig and Marilee for helping mum and dad deliver leaflets and newspapers around the Hays in Craigmillar during the YES campaign in 2014. Sorry we didn't win this time kids but, the fight for independence will go on. When Alex signed Craig's flag he wrote a message saying "KEEP THE FLAG FLYING". We tried to give you, Craig, Mari and Charlie, a better future in Scotland. Keep fighting.
Love Mum and Dad xxx

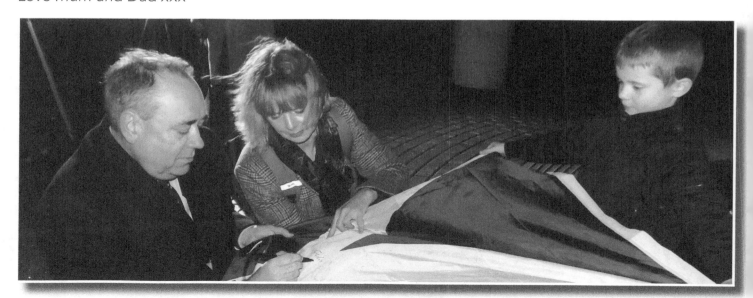

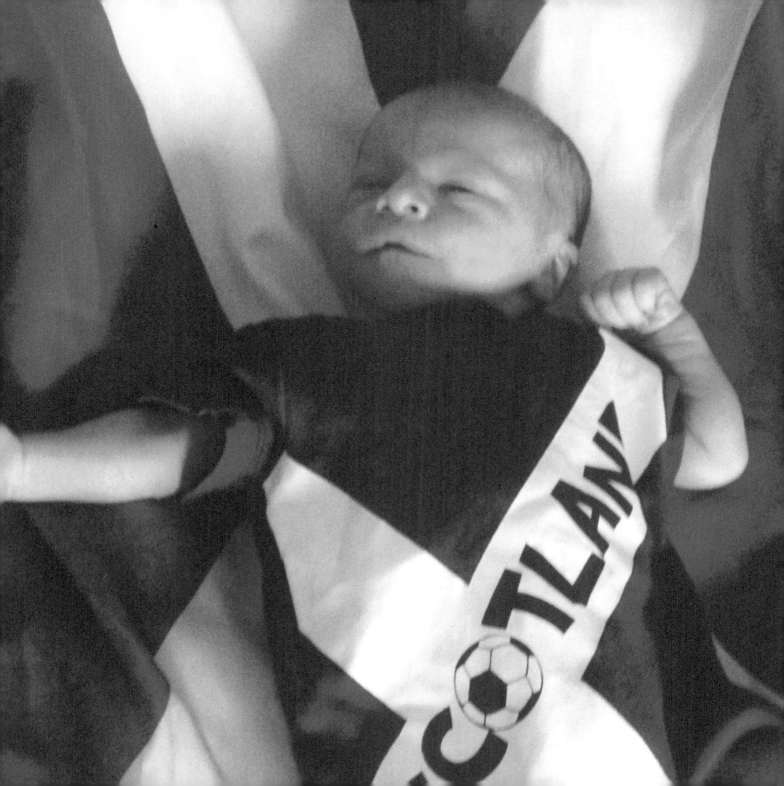

WEE WARRIORS.

Dione and Rhea,
my brave wee warriors.
Mummy and Daddy
love you both.

*Liam & Lily Kinnaird,
we are so proud of you for
showing hope over fear!
Remember these days as it will
be your generation who shapes
the future of our Bonnie land,
love mum and dad xx*

Sonny

*I hope that one day
we are free,
Grasping the future
like your YES at age 3.*

Love Mum xx

*Hope, love, peace,
faith and freedom.
You make me so proud
my 5 wee Scottish warriors.
Love mum
xxxxx*

THE SMILES O' OOR SCOTTISH PRINCESSES.

Summer, you're my world and I fight for my country but most of all for your future to be bright and wonderful. I love you to the moon and back, you're my little freedom fighter! Mummy xx

To our beautiful daughter Isla.

We did this for you and hope one day to all come back, celebrating a yes vote.

Love, mummy and daddy.

Amelia,

Sorry baby, I tried.

Love mum xxx

Don't worry
it's just a delay -
we will be
independent soon

I promise
xxx

So proud of you Shaun,

a real Scottish boy
through and through,
hope over fear!!

Love Michelle xxx

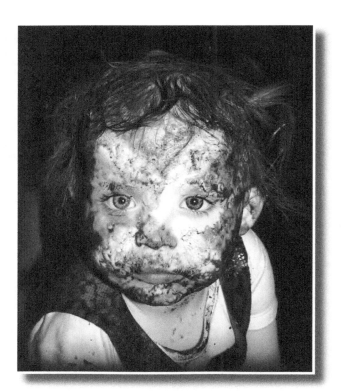

Kayleigh,

you and all other children are the
future of Scotland,
never give up on hope !!
Saor alba.

Love mum xxx

To Mhairi and Freya

You won the hearts of many with your dedication to the cause.
The dream will never die.
Scotland is proud of you.

Love Mum, xxx

Dear Hayden,

we are lucky to have you here today.

Love mum and Dad x

Sending all our love to our family and friends in Uddingston, Scotland from Philadelphia, PA, USA

Dear Euan,

You can be anything you want to be, I hope you can one day lead Scotland into the future, because I gave you wings to fly higher than I ever did.

I love you
Saor Alba xx

DIGITAL ECHOES.
by Mark Barnes

Nicholas, we are so proud of you... Love you always, Mum and Dad. x

I tweeted, I posted, I liked and I shared,
but nobody followed, nobody cared.
I uploaded my pains and hoped they'd go viral,
instead I was plummeted down in a spiral.

My digital echoes were buried in bits,
covered by dust of youtube greatest hits.
Life can be funny, when you're not feeling pain,
Let's hope we all learn to enjoy life again.

This digital graveyard we're building so fast,
blink and it's gone, and what of our past.
What are we leaving our children behind,
#NothingOfSubstance for them to find.

The digital vaults and passwords galore,
Will cease to exist, a bolted cage door.
The treasure within, silenced and sad,
Lost out to a battle with some silly fad.

Our children are drowning in a torrent of stuff,
But we're hiding importance and feeding them fluff.
They'll never know patience, or kindness or joy,
While we instantly gratify this internet toy.

My digital essence is fleeting for sure,
I can edit the past, keeping it pure,
No-one will know the journey I took,
It was silently changed in a digital book.

The ether engulfs us, we notice no more,
We buy goods online, so what of the store,
We never meet people, we Skype them online,
We're happy with this, oh yes, we are fine.

But when we are lonely, or sad, or depressed,
Will kind Mr Zuckerberg help you get dressed,
You gave him your life, your hopes and your dreams,
But he prefers cash, at least that's how it seems.

So go on and tweet, post, like and share,
I hope you find someone who will really care,
Not for the facade, or what you present,
But for the hidden, secret and deadly torment.

They'll know you and get you, they'll pull at your heart,
A life that's worth living will get a kickstart,
You'll ditch all the gadgets and gizmos with glee,
And say to yourself – "I'm happy I'm me".

NoMoreHiding.me/2014/09/digital-echoes/

Don't let go of hope!!!

DECLARATION OF ARBROATH.
by Kayleigh Nelson

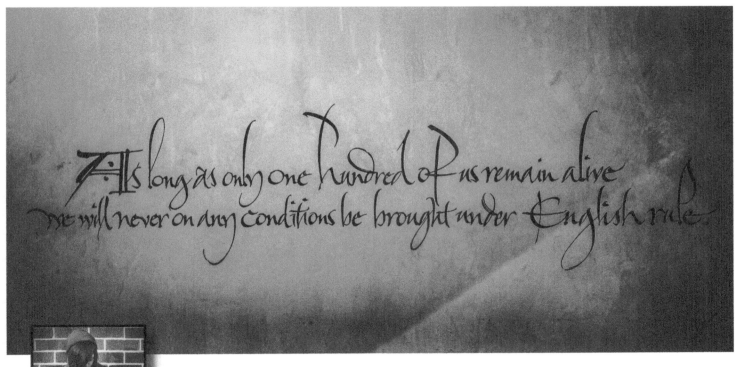

"As a design engineer, I have always been drawn towards creative pursuits and problem solving. From scribbling with crayons on the pavement to a recent leap into photography. In discovering the art of photography, I have enjoyed sharing my creations with the world. This photograph was taken in Edinburgh whilst visiting the National Museum of Scotland, it highlights the heart and spirit, if not the will, of the Scottish people."

This book would not have been possible without the generous help, support and donations from some of the most wonderful people. I thank each and every one who contributed from the bottom of my heart. I also thank each and every person who supported me while I compiled this, in particular my wonderful wife, Michaela Barnes.

I tried diligently to source and credit the originator of everything used in the book, but there are certain items included where the originator couldn't be traced or crediting would distract from the content. It was important to include some of these to demonstrate the impact that social media had in the campaigns. The Scottish referendum demonstrated that the fight for democracy is finding new and exciting ways to challenge the propaganda generated by government, corporations and media.

This book is your book. It is but a snapshot of a moment in time. This was your moment in time. Thank you for sharing your moments with me.   Thank you for allowing me to share them with the world.

My heart is, and always will be, with Scotland.

Alba gu bràth

There are a few people who deserve special recognition for their contribution.
In no particular order they would be: Ivon Bartholomew, Stephen McBride,
Scoturk Design, Keyser Soze, Byzantine K and Trebor Anderson.

SCOTURK
DESIGN

Lightning Source UK Ltd.
Milton Keynes UK
UKOW07n0622191115

263065UK00003B/11/P